When I think of a Spirograph I see interlocking and repeating patterns, distinctive colours overlapping, a pleasing symmetry. When I try and draw one I ~~~ udges, the lines blur.

I started writing ι although some of the poen I was co-editing Magma 7. asked to do this because a l ~~~ are about work. I have been a drug and alcohol nurse for years; a job I love but the conditions, for all concerned, are frustrating. There are many stories to be told about this but I can only write from my own perspective and my main concern is to avoid appropriating other people's experience, while wanting to give an account of something which is hardly written about from this angle. I also like writing about landscapes and hidden, mostly female, histories. This is the origin of the first three sections of the book. The last section is called wonder, which is open to interpretation. Everything is aspirational.

I hope you enjoy the poems.

Spirograph

Pauline Sewards

Burning Eye

Supported using public funding by ARTS COUNCIL ENGLAND

LOTTERY FUNDED

This edition published by Burning Eye Books 2020

www.burningeye.co.uk

@burningeyebooks

Burning Eye Books
15 West Hill, Portishead, BS20 6LG

ISBN 978-1-911570-93-6

October 2020

To Helen

Spirograph

with love and gratitude
for all your poetic
wisdom and inspiration

Pauline
xx

For Maisie, Ethel Amelia and Annie
my mother and grandmothers

CONTENTS

WORK

AFTER BURNOUT

I'm going back to work next week,
one hand on my policies
and *The Little Book of Mindfulness*.
The other hand clutching my pen,
which in my mind
has swelled to cartoon proportions.

My mother worked for three decades
at a newsagent's in Market town,
ironed her uniform every morning,
cursed, 'Nylon's a sod for creases,'
over the hissing steam.

She wore a badge saying Happy to Help.
I'm in the helping business too,
although the word is so loaded
I don't know what it means any more.
The newsagent's closed ten years ago,
pigeons crap in the gutters,
net curtains grey in the windows.

Stories have spun themselves
while I've been away.
Red alerts on the screen
will demand data.

My mother is a survivor.
When she walks around Market town
she's greeted as a minor celebrity.
'I remember buying my Mirror from you.
You always had a smile.'

I walk on broken glass.
My pen is the means of production.

HOW DO YOU SHIFT DEPRESSION?

You turn it into concrete
and chisel its face slowly.

You name all of its parts,
sadness
grief
envy
rage
shame,

and own them as you own your hair
or your fingernails
or the dance you make through the world.

You sit by the water and listen.
Suspend disbelief
like a tightrope to tiptoe your dreams.

You breathe
until your heart is open
those simple things
no one taught you.

THIRTEEN DAYS IN

What gets you out of bed in the morning?

A colleague, whose name I've learned but can't yet spell,
reports that clients are smoking Spice down in the lobby.

We are two floors up in the two-thirds empty
ex-council building with a permanently out-of-action lift.

We look out over derelict docklands
through crazed glass windows like broken lace.

Rafter bones poke from smashed skulls
of once-proud red brick warehouses.

Rubble makes dust of flattened lots
where high-rise lives were taken down.

Maria breezes in on a mission between jobs,
says she isn't clean yet, has to keep earning.

Her face is ash grey, gappy smile, blouse unbuttoned to her bra,
ponytail tied so tight her eyebrows are permanently raised, ready
for business.

What are your goals? Where do you see yourself in six months'
time?

Maria points at a tower of sticks and rubbish
two floors below, ready for Bonfire Night.

'Maybe there'll be fireworks,' she says.

A colleague says, 'Be careful. She talks too much
as a smokescreen to avoid answering questions.'

Are you injecting? Which drugs have you used in the last five days?

Maria says she would never actively try and kill herself
but sometimes feels like she can't be arsed to stay alive.

At 5pm it's almost dark; we hurry to leave, go down in pairs for
    safety.
The lobby smells of burnt rubber and fish glue.

ASSESSMENT

This is the social contract.
I will ask you twenty questions
and respond with solutions
while simultaneously typing
your answers, make eye contact
with my screen as I winnow
literal from emotional truth
and sometimes lies.

But I lie too; when asked
I say, 'I'm fine.' But I'm rapidly
getting behind with my notes
and *nothing that happens
happens if it isn't in the notes.*

In the last century we had
how long? Three hours,
three days to do the work
of thirty minutes today.
One after another, back to back.
No reflective space.
No slack time
for healthy social contact.

DRUG SERVICE

Sites

mark this diagram
with an X
at all the places
you inject
arms legs hands
running out of veins
going
in the groin now
where the
femoral artery
and nerve
are a shiver
from the mainline
going
in the neck
where
the carotid artery
throbs

Needle Exchange

I offer you foil packed in shiny slabs
like stacks of empty chocolate bars
but you say you'll never go back to smoking
although you hate needles with a vengeance.
The bin you return is splashed with blood.
I issue a new one the colour of a child's sun,
twenty sets of works in a stripy paper bag.

Harm Reduction

He's collecting needles for Christmas, blues,
long greens, short oranges and sachets of citric.

I pack them inside a four-litre sin bin,
double-bag to disguise as Tesco shopping.

In exchange for a urine sample
and a long, hard blow into a breathalyser,
I issue a fortnight script to tide him over.
'Negative, except prescribed, and zero.'
'I know,' he says. 'I've not been using.'
'Have a good holiday.' 'I will,' he says, and winks,
signs his name on the record, next to mine.

Sample

It's a busy morning.
One hand shakes hello;
the other hands out a urine pot.
I'm writing case notes in my head.
Sometimes I forget to smile
or I use the word clean
when I mean opiate-free.

The clinic has been turned
into a testing room.
They've built a toilet in the corner,
installed air conditioning
to keep the kit in perfect nick.
I peel back the label to read the result:
morphine, cocaine, methadone,
the story of her week.

Treatment

If I could give you a house I would.
If I could teach you to read I would.
If I could mend your childhood I would.
If I could mend your broken spine I would.
If I could change the law I would.

If I could get him to stop abusing you I would.
If I could find the respect you deserve I would.
If I could mend the cuts I would.
If I had any change I would.

ROCHE RUMBLE

Some sing in vibrant shades.
I praise women who live in beige.

Thrifty shoppers in market halls
who never want to stand out at all.

Mothers with pale, wrinkled faces,
same shade and texture as their fleeces.

Women who've suffered years of trauma
relieved to live days of P&Q

in flats with fitted kitchen goods,
carpet, curtains, cushions, rugs

made in a blandly oatmeal hue
the Shopping Channel labels taupe.

I praise women who've earned their beige,
cuddle inside its muted hug

(my sister in her closing weeks
content blank behind her eyes)

but hope one day the scales will rise,
lift the benzodiazepine daze,

faintest blue will shimmer through,
mossy green, a fizz of mauve, then hot cerise,

the world in its melting colours raise,
sunlight slat venetian blinds.

THE WOMAN NEXT DOOR

She was – riding a bicycle into her eighties.
She was – knowing all the news in her hometown even when
　　she moved a hundred miles away.
She was – always wearing a headscarf, knotted under her chin.
She was – dewy face, silk blouse and marcel wave. Soft-lipped
　　and pretty at sixteen.
She was – never as diligent as her mother, at housework, thrift
　　and caring for the sick, had no skill for knitting, embroidery
　　or growing flowers.

She was – never good enough for her husband, with his sharp
　　suit, Brylcreemed hair and shiny smile. He had stepped
　　down a few rungs of the social ladder to marry her, and
　　never let her forget it.
She was – unable to celebrate her wedding anniversary
　　because the date was a giveaway to the timing of her
　　pregnancy.

She was – a hoarder of newspaper clippings, knick-knacks,
　　descaler of kettles, obsessed with pulling spider hair from
　　plug holes.
She was – wearing the same brown tweed skirt year in, year
　　out.
She was – never going out with her husband.
She was – revelling in his absence, reclining on the sofa.
She was – three people in her marriage.
She was – grown thin, hollow-eyed and silent.

She was – knotted wool to unravel.
She was – blue like her brother's eyes and drab like her
　　overcoat.

She was – sofa-surfing at her sons', homeless at eighty-five.
She was – finally broken from the charming rat trap of coercive
　　control.

She was – laying her hand on your arm whenever she had you
in the room.
Spilling out her story in one breath, leaving no space to
interrupt her.

MOLLY

i.m. Jason Molina

You are the gig we can never go to now,
Songs: Ohia – live!

Hymning America before the lights go out,
strumming foundries and factories
with riffs and beats.

Poet of the working man,
hold up your guitar and fist,
John Henry split my heart.

Jason, with your ketone breath, your dispositions,
stayed hungry and in tune.

Pencilled fresh lines on old envelopes
as, behind the power station,
the sickle moon slipped down,
crooked, smiling.

SPARK BOY

tells narratives in an onion skin
knew a highway
salt-scoured and lit white
he was a Steiff bear
button in ear authentic
his new skin
soft as kid leather unmarked
unremarkable
he wore his shadow side
as a skull ring
his scars like priceless trash
he is so young
and will stay young
begging for charity and clarity
leaves to dodge
where night is a lurch church of bruises
warns
the West End is a fish tank
of iPhones and iPads and iPockets

BACK THEN

A building centuries old, listed, white walls,
low beams riddled with treated woodworm.
Tiny rooms with bang-your-forehead door arches.
Ye Olde Red Lion etched faintly on the windows.

It wasn't the building that mattered
as much as the fact that it was thought worthwhile
to have it open and welcoming
five days a week and late on Tuesdays.

Ye Olde Red Lion is protected by planning regs,
but the alcohol service is limited and somewhere else,
the counselling rooms are empty,
ghosts hallucinate optics and bars.

FIREWATER

He knew the whisky would kill him – not the beer, mild and bitter, of the earth, not the benign small beer drunk by his forebears, which put a song on their lips and a smile, keeping them mellow, training them to carry the yoke without complaint.

He knew the whisky would kill him, not words. Though he feared words once when they battered him with names. Words were his power; in daily cryptic crosswords his memory stretched from Shakespeare to Ginsberg. His wit was terse and sweet.

Whisky got to his liver. They found it in the fire, a pickled walnut, but his heart and soul were there too. Two pigeons still beating their wings against the buckled window glass.

Whisky sent him comatose, slipped the cigarette from his languorous fingers, setting off the papers that filled the room, creeping an outline up and down the bookshelf stairs. Did he wake early? The warmth on his face like the breath of a lover, then the light ruddy as hell. Did he hear the crackling sound and think, *That description's not a cliché after all*?

Did he get to reach out for that steadying glass before the smoke snuffed life from his lungs? I hope so.

FARWELTERED

We set off early as the hills were so far away.
Collected 'scripts' the day before.
Stopped for garage sandwiches and cans of Lilt.
Roads got narrower, steeper, more winding.
Dagger needed a piss, so we stopped in a layby;
someone shouted, 'Take a plastic pot with you,
in case they want a sample.'

When we arrived the full heat of the day
was still held back by hazy clouds.
The Brecon Beacons were blue in the distance;
we breathed clean air and silence.
Even our cynical ears could not detect the sound of traffic.
We walked slowly, dodging nettles, brambles and gorse,
paused for restorative cigarettes.

Dagger spotted it first,
lying amongst cow parsley and white campion
in the dried-up ditch.
Fleece grubby below a cloud of buzzing flies,
four legs sticking up above the bloated belly,
a blood-rank smell.
Compelling drama of nothing happening.

We gathered round and watched
and watched each other watching.
Loz said it was disgusting, turned her stomach,
but she could handle it, she'd seen far worse.
Barry, who never said much,
talked about working in a butcher's shop,
the skills he learnt, respect for the knife.
The animal was silent.

A farmer arrived by tractor,
got on with the grim job of moving the carcass.
On the way home we joked
the highlight of the day had been

not the stunning view or garage sandwiches
but the sheep and the way it made us feel
to see it lying on its back,
gone too far over. Stuck.

DAY'S WORK

sideswipe on a Monday morning
a sting in the ear phone call hit his brain like a poisoned dart
she's gone over the voice told him through the static

mad girl she'd been running a risky duet with death
for a decade complacency had set in
he thought survival begat survival somehow she'd come back

from whatever party the weekend twisted her through
not true – bent through hoops her heart beating in two directions
lungs drowning in their own secretions

one finger typing the tick box Datex all morning
grown man weeping
tattooed burly head in hands

no time to mourn the frail feisty bones
a litany of loss a negative statistic adverse outcome
tears wiped on his sleeve

IVYDEAN

Who will tribute these women?
Trapped in the aspic of the seventies

while punk rock rages outside
and Thatcher waits ghoulishly in the wings.

Trapped in the locked ward
where iron beds line up in Victorian bays

on concrete and marble floors
and window restrictors hold in stale air.

They toe the Largactil shuffle
as student nurses wash their hair

with cheap strawberry shampoo,
share stories as water drains into the sink.

Who will tribute these women?
I no longer have their real names.

Rosemary for remembrance,
third eye drawn on her forehead
in lipstick and kohl.

Maureen with the silk kimono
who stabbed her husband as he was sleeping,
no other way to slay the beast
who beat her head against the wall,

and Judy Blue Eyes,
survivor of two hundred and six sessions
of electroconvulsive therapy.

WHERE

MY BRISTOL ISN'T THE SAME AS YOURS BUT I BET IT OVERLAPS

I don't spend all my days eating Pieminister,
shopping for vintage in Stokes Croft
and photographing Banksys,
although sometimes I do.

And I haven't been to the bridge for years
to admire the view,
although I once met a woman
who jumped from it and survived.

My Bristol is the snowy day
that surprised us when we first arrived
from the North. It is the kids
sledging on tea trays at Narroways.

It is a tangle of all the paths
I've walked since then.
Work at the harbour and Blackberry Hill.
Learning to drive in Fishponds.

Drinking coffee in Kino, music at the Cube.
Ashton Court Free Festival.
My Bristol is a list poem
with more unticked than I'll ever do.

When the kids were small
I lived Bristol vicariously through Venue,
and when they grew up
they delivered Bristol to me via DIY culture.

Now they've gone I tread my own stages;
every night is something new.
Bristol is billboard poems on the corner,
the taste of fresh onion bhajis from Sonni's.

It is the view of Dundry's green hill
as I travel home on the M32.
A city small enough to see the other side of
but with no limits that I know of.

HANDS OFF STOKES CROFT

Stop this brutal gentrification, daily process, slow-creep
jerk-stepped infiltration of our loved shabby streets.
With bland wash, glazed panes, sleek steel,
wobbly fonts mimicking homespun vernacular.
Taking down the car spray metallic, buzz-cut signage,
breaching Turbo Island and the cellophane flower shrine
of love to Jama.
Leave these streets.

Their side-to-side
sambuca shot shambles.
Send Rita's curry chips as mail art.
Prefer a white paper bag of fresh pakoras
to a slate-plated jus-splattered steak.
Saw off Meat Liquor's co-option
of art deco lines of the heating shop.

Now the offshore investors pick, pick, pick at the bones
of Hamilton house, development by stealth.
Leave this jumble ferment, car horn, sound jangle,
Take Five all-nighters, Crofters Rights.
Silver-threaded hand-knitted jackets hug lampposts by
    Nine Tree Hill.

DUB LEGEND

sequinned and gee-gawed   glittering psychosis   thumb
nose ganja strike

wilful bird   weary, weary   pink heart kisses cascade on
3D plastic baseball cap

become boy again, running in vine-creep meadows nettles
running deep two step sway

henna flesh   drink deep ginger wine dub legend dub icon

deep down voice   hug break like a bird   sings of ashes
and six foot six

we are love and awe   raise flash of gimcrack bracelet sweet
smoke banana

crowd current sway waves   fix eyes to face lift hands

dub echo   dub dub heartbeat   ivy veins cling immortal
        rooted fire

FOR JAZZMAN JOHN

You flowed through the city with your poems in your hands,
embodied enthusiasm, bebopped a river; you guided me
to Glitterbeast and Beat, always sharing words and stories,
the place to be and the way to be in the place. I remember
your Thinking Cap at 93 Feet East, Talking Rhythm, Festibelly
when you gave in to campsite roughing it, loved a massage
in the healing tent, swapped poems for mugs of tea and pasta.
Totally owned not only stage but the goddamn field around it.
Oh man, I didn't know you well, but I was proud to know you.
I looked for you in every basement upstairs room. I rode beside
you on the all-night bus, hugged you every time we met.
I loved your news and enthusiasm, washed up in your face,
your iconic, beloved carrier bags. Positively Jazzman, miss you so.

VISITING THE CHELSEA HOTEL

we walk along the Hudson river climb
onto the highline where monarchs swarm
purple verbenas and dry grass
cross block on block heart in mouth
walk don't walk yellow taxi traffic horns
count down the numbers on west 25
spot the red brick high rise one time
'world's tallest building'

ventilator shaft intubates basement window
the building pegged by scaffolding breathes
like an asthmatic old man
tarnished plaques eulogise counterculture heroes
Burroughs Thomas Cohen Warhol

we search for traces of Patti and Janis
find only these damp bones
silt of cockroach wings stink of hooch
then glimpse awkwardly from fenced-off steps
in corridors soaked with yellow light
pale shapes on walls where art once hung

ICE AND OCEAN

i
Water will find its own shape,
        running through open gutters,
down narrow streets,
        between soft gas lights and harsh voices,
running into that hard place
        your fingers found,
breathing blue chemical tang
        in pre-dawn light.
When the sun broke through   striated clouds
        it was blood
leaking a thin trickle from choked gills.

ii
This town always was a war zone,
        one whisky away from
a broken bottle thrust to the face.

On the front page a smiling lad
        could be a bridegroom, father, hero footballer,
but instead he's the victim,
        one hundred and seventy-nine separate injuries.

This town could be any town
        mugged by cuts
and county lines.

iii
1950 lingers in the café,
        in the waitress's apron,
        the logo on the leather placemats
        and the silver fish knives
        weighty and safe as charms.

iv
Ice and Ocean:
town of the death card dealers
        where every man once had two homes,
        one on land and the other on sea.

Where families came second only to rum
        and were run by the matriarch
        who had all her teeth removed at twenty-one,
        a present to make her more marriageable.
        Now she shares ectoplasm jelly
        with her great-grandchildren.

v
Ice:
        the ice factory churned twenty-four hours a day.
        Gas turned water into rocks
        to preserve shoals of fish captured at sea.
        In cold weather the water looks like steam
        rising from frosty haunches.

Soon haddock will be rare as dragon.

vi
Ocean:
in Solly's café every meal
like every voyage
        could be the last,
        fish so fresh it twitched on the plate,
        white bread and butter,
        chlorophyll peas,
farewell.
        Lace curtains still at the windows now,
        the sailor boys linger
        behind the padlocked door,
a litany of smiles,
farewell.

vii
A knee-trembler in the ginnel
against the crumbling wall;
      fingers that remember the feel
      of hair
      pulled tight to deepen kisses
      will learn to fasten complicated ropes
      and later freeze to bone.
      Fathoms deep.
The trawler sails on;
commerce waited for no man
and then it was gone.

viii
I dream of a lost girl
waiting in the alleyways at the edge of the docks,
thin dress beneath her leopardskin coat.
Her friend Kit promises
the red tulips of spring will arrive soon.

I am told no local would ever use
the word *kasbah*
for this tumbling maze of brick.

In my dreams I am tiny.
I dive deep, deep into the pickle jar.

ATTITUDE

this is the last Fall gig
the bitter fig the twisted cig the rig unrigged
in the stone clink
with the first Fall fan ankle tattoo like biro twigs

no rock no punk no polish no spin no spit

boy in a white shirt
boy in a woolly jumper
rider in two carrier bags
unlikely provider of the last Fall gig
built wheelchair ramp and safe den
on the high stage

queue overlaps around the block
round the stone clink
after the thousand thousand thousand shows
this is no show

sends unlikely love to the empty stage
boy in a white shirt
boy in a woolly jumper

everyone will say they were there but you weren't there either

fans overlap around the block
what will we do now?

spun out and suddenly older
spun out and suddenly older

PRIDE

Mary says she didn't know what a rainbow flag was
until a woman with a glorious voice raised one at the Albert
Hall.

'She said she was *just a fat queer from Kansas,*' Mary says
with love and wonder in her voice.

Like all of Mary's conversations this is repeated a lot,
like turns of a hamster wheel over and over.

She couples it with the comments that made her feel sick,
complaints of bias by 'appalled', 'outraged' and 'offended'

who hated the way jingoism at the Prom was tempered
by music titled 'Woke' and 'For Democracy',

hated most that tiny smiling woman who enunciated every
    syllable
and opened her scarlet mouth to let her voice out on wings.

Mary says she knows what Blake meant when he wrote
    'Jerusalem',
that it isn't for the Union Jacks and the Brexiters.
She calls him William Morris by mistake, but she's utterly
sincere.

Repeats herself so much, can hardly get out of her sitting
room,
where not a lot happens except on TV.
Mary's granddaughter thinks she repeats her stories
because they are telling something she can't directly say.

A memory of when news was whispered adult conversations,
valve radios broadcasting sonorous voices,
rumours of Kristallnacht and jackboots, gas masks, blackout
    curtains,
screeching sirens, spitfires crossing miles of sky.

As leaves fall from the trees
Mary watches the Prom with her granddaughter.
A vase of gladioli comes into bloom like lipstick flowers,
and Jamie Barton hits that high note,
somewhere over the rainbow.

WHO

PREMONITION/HINDSIGHT

see that girl in the photograph
gamine in black and white
the blurry edges almost
hide
her awkwardness
she's cross-legged and you can't tell
that her skirt is corduroy
her jacket outsized
she's channelling one part Audrey Hepburn
one part Annie Hall
her crooked smile is hidden
as always beneath closed lips
but she does look happy
even carefree
and I want to reach into the photograph
and grab her shake her
shake her like a rag doll
take her away from this place
or better still
get her to leave of her own accord
say don't do it escape now
say to her that although you may do good work
that uniform will always make you sweat
and you will never keep that stupid paper
hat fixed to your head
it's a noble profession
but not for you
others can do it
and only you
can write our poems and stories
I want to whisper into her shell-like
where the silver earring dangles
I want to shout

don't let yourself become that square peg
forever
shaving off essential corners
to fit imperfectly into that round hole
I want to shout
this is dangerous because you are not
rigorous and obsessed enough
not as methodical as you pretend to be

you are a dreamer
a diver for pearls
you will work hard but you will surely end up in debt
trying to quell the daily anxieties
which jitter through your heart
that girl in the photograph
doesn't know the world will eat her
from the inside out
she has no courage
no sense of talent or self-worth
she lives long ago
before the stage was just another corner of the floor
and everyone had to be their own personal
publicity machine
she will read her poems one day
but by then she'll be wearing another body
heavier wrinkled the hair white at the roots
she will be herself and not herself
it will almost be time for her to hand herself in
I want to reach into the photograph
say listen to your heart
take the green lane of the imagination
and run

MOTHER'S DAY AT ROLL FOR THE SOUL

We don't know each other, but our daughters are intimates.
They have held each other's hair and shared cubicles we can
    never enter,
but at one time or another we've all given sofa space to each
    other's girls,
been a confidant, heard stories we'll never retell.

We meet for the first time on this day when we are invited
to share the pinnacle of their lives.

One mum wears skinny denim and multiple badges.
I don't realise she's dressed up for the occasion and think she
    always looks this way.
The other, like me, shows her nerves and fizzing excitement;
she drinks too much coffee – I gulp beer from a bottle,
keen to look as cool as a middle-aged mum in an indie café
    can be.

When the time comes for our performance it's so tender –
the way each young woman beckons us to shadow her,
    drummer
        keyboard
            vocals.
We occupy our stations, obedient as children,
and when we take it from the top of the feminist anthem
we joyously settle scores with our raised voices.

In the future the café goes dark,
there are geographical and musical differences,
and we may never again be together in the same room, in the
    same city,

but it will always be true
that we were on the guest list.
Sharing the stage.
Shouting, 'I will destroy you,'
and feeling creative and free.

SWIMMING IN THE WOMEN'S POND

Ride the 24 from Pimlico to Hampstead Heath.
Cycle the superhighway and turn right at Islington.
Leave the road at the Vale of Health, walk
ankle-deep in grass, squeeze in bramble alley

to the hidden gate. Pay in honesty coins,
flat foot wooden boards in changing rooms,
grab towel, cold shower . Queue to launch
shivering body naked into tingling haven.

Drench parched city skin, propel and glide
deep below green hair of duckweed.
Be aware of body, swim decorously,
avoid clumsy clashes, splash only in fun.

Afterwards soak sun on crowded blankets,
exposed in the grass slopes' heat shimmer,
screened by dense hedges from voyeuristic gaze.
Consider the sisters who founded this place.

Tough women who shimmied out of stiff petticoats.
Made ripples become unstoppable waves.

PLAYROOM

Kissing cousins coupled twin-land

twisted this singleton into keep-net

to sail across linoleum in stockinged feet

build treasure islands from driftwood

and shivering sea glass

lick salt from long brined chessmen

rub crystal globe for history of shipwrecks

Squinted light

renders us entirely underwater

where the old man sailor strokes his beard

salvaged in stories

a worn-out deck of cards

iron thumb ring fashioned from an anchor

WEDNESDAY PLAY

Three-piece suite positioned in front of a small TV.

My parents sit each side of me and I hide my face with my hair
during the embarrassing parts. Which is all of it.
I focus on peeling an orange, inching the thick skin,
white pith, transparent membranes. I note how the pulp is
    packed
into tiny cases. I eat slowly, with my eyes first.
On screen there is sex. 'Things are turning peculiar,' my father
    says.
Sometimes I pick a blood orange by mistake,
force down its crime scene surprise with my eyes closed.
Sometimes there is a baby orange inside my orange.
A navel, my mother overexplains.

Onscreen the action rolls on in black and white. No one moves
    until
the clock strikes nine and my dad says he will make the tea.
With the air of a monarch dispensing favours
he brings in the tray, three cups slopping into saucers,
a bowl of sugar, a plate of butterfly cakes and sliced fruit loaf.
At last the credits roll, Dennis Potter or Stephen Poliakof.
I have eaten all of my fruit, even the pith and peel.

AT KATRINA'S HOUSE

terrapins were the pets from outer space
matchbox fit to open palms
bead-size heads and claws a mere stitch
striped legs poking out of keratin carapace
cute yet carnivorous
jaws devoured bloody steak
and spumed fudgy chains
into the blue waters of their Sputnik-shaped tank
she couldn't picture them among
her parents' mahogany veneers
but here at Katrina's house they were at home
among the plastic ribbon curtains
dusty tinned coffee powder
and a mother who wore a baby doll nightie
beneath her housecoat
and fluffy mules with a silver heel

THE TOWN ABUSER

His shadow infiltrates Market town, cowers us still.
The shocking thing is that it happened over and over again.
The shocking thing is that everyone knew
and women have said, 'Me too,' not fiercely but with rueful
    laughter.

We were just girls in white ankle socks,
some of us overburdened at the top, even in primary school.
He was red face, loud voice, spider-leg hairs
on the backs of his fingers.

I dodged him by keeping the desk between us.
Looking back, he could still have pounced on me,
but he saved his paws for juicier prey,
although he bullied me in public;
once he hit my head with a blackboard rubber
to 'prove my skull was thinner than a native's'.

After his massive heart attack he retired.
But a collective sigh of relief was extinguished
when he Lazarused as a supply teacher.
Slimmed down, blue-tinged, less blustery, courting sympathy.
Still spreading his legs when he sat at the front of the classroom,
leeringly ordering us to solve complex multiplications.
A long stretch up in a short skirt
to write the answers with crumbling chalk.

Fifty years later I'm in my friend's shop on a sunny day –
a Market-town cave of bric-a-brac, Nepalese saris and crystals.
The once junior maths teacher has parked his mobility scooter
and spills antique beans about his fellow school teachers.

He says some were nice, some drank their lives away, and
    some were
sinister. Turns out there wasn't one abuser but many,
the head teacher's wife, the auctioneer, the police, the Freemasons
all in on it. All in on it.

This is such a familiar story, but this is Market town.
And I have known some of it. And I have been silent.

SOMETHING WICKED THIS WAY COMES

Leafed on dank, dead afternoons, drew graphite gardens on Formica. So much love for the flop-haired nice guy, fringe over black frames, hip to hip behind the counter sweatshop between the Mr Whippy machine and the phallic poutings of the still. Served weak tea, separated mouse ephemera from oyster wafers.

Cookie-cutter girls had easy lives; belonged to the first teams, healthy as Scholl foot care, as a glass and half, fresh petals with smooth axilla.

Collect eyes like library tickets, Gatsby eyes, the boy-man's eyes half-green, half-violet – myopic – saw a demon's eyes in embossed flock. Clinched cartoon arms, fungal glow of fresh tattoos.

Met at right angles, no glances exchanged, all that loose change spilled on the counter. Net cloth in hand to look busy, discussed immaculate imported vinyl.

Changed shifts, left town. Remember, in rare conjunction of candyfloss and Buffalo Springfield, scars on steam-scalded fingers.

NARNIA UNIVERSITY

Autumn trees reflected head-first in the lakes. Brilliance
by the turreted hall where we would discuss Marx and RD Laing.
New arrivals at Stoke station were directed to the free bus to
    campus
run by Potteries Motor Transport – shortened to PMT – giggles
    for no reason.
The first real student I saw was the girl with long red hair;
she wore love beads and a plaid shirt, we all wanted to be her.
I made friends with a girl on my corridor. We mixed Horlicks
    with water
in the communal kitchen. Pretended we weren't homesick,
torn from our comfort zones, hearts as raw as chicks.

'You've never been abroad?' a braying girl said to me
during a tutorial. I felt impossible as a dodo, mud on a carpet.
But a couple of weeks later she confessed that she had slept
    with *that* guy –
the one who walked around shirtless showing off his yoga body.
I pictured him, white denim jeans, his bare feet treading the
    grass,
wondered why she'd come to me to ask if this was 'genius or a
    terrible mistake'.

The professor conducted sociology tutorials cross-legged on a
    cushion.
He once walked off the stage from a lecture straight into a
    cupboard.
Realising his mistake, he listened for the stampede of departing
    students
followed by a hush. Thinking it safe, he opened the door and
    stepped out …
but the whole audience was still seated. Some clever dick
had seen the error, mimed like a conductor, to fake the students
leaving.

MY GRANDMOTHERS

were one-liners
two-worders
non-speaking parts
tiptoeing trays
into dining rooms
rising before dawn
to riddle ashes
walking home
in too-tight boots
on high days
and holidays
bleeding into rags
in secret closets

my grandmothers
were stitchers
daisy chain and purl
they were
'only women's work'
unwritten poems
stories told
as mere gossip
they were young once
blushy and bosomy
discovered and undone

my grandmothers
brewed bitter remedies
read headlines
and heartlines
remembered a time
before bunions
and arthritic handshakes
left recipes instead of diaries
went to their graves
with gold rings
still gleaming
in soft earlobes
their secrets bagged
in white cotton shrouds

JULY

July should be strawberries,
green fields turning gold,
blue skies leavened white
by clouds and shrieking seagulls.

But you fell headlong
on the level floor,
slipped into a whirl
of sheets and tissues,

noxious smells, beeping alarms,
dry food and weak tea.
Your hands and body bruised
from needles and infusions.

Your broken ribs were like snapped
matchsticks as conflicting treatments
for embolism and pneumothorax
fought fluid and clots.

A risky tube was inserted into your ribs
after you signed the Respect care plan
(resuscitation unlikely to be successful
as advanced in age and frail).

You dreamt of a face-off
between Trump and Kim Jong Un,
each with a finger on The Button.
'Stupid fools,' you shouted.

'Don't you realise you'll both die too?'
It was quiet when you woke,
rare peace on the ward at 5am.
You believed the apocalypse had come.

Flies cluster on fennel,
that aniseed smell, stubble burns
in your memories
of summers long ago.

ALL MY ANCESTORS HAVE A GHOST STORY

Told like a calling card in the candle's wobbly light.
An old man met in the woods
asks for help with his burden of kindling
but he's dead already and six feet under.
The tom cat's green-eyed, blazing stare
raises prickles on the nape of my grandmother's neck
before he runs right through the bedroom wall.

Tonight, in a room which smells of apples and pine,
you tell me your granddaughter is four
and remembers another life, on an island of women,
remembers her own death
from cannon fire at the age of eight.
You say she acts like an old soul,
like an older child, running ahead of herself,
gathering herbs to dry for the winter.

I riposte with the photo of my grand-greats
wearing stern, corrugated faces,
deep-dyed Sunday clothes.
'Stare hard,' I say, and your gasp tells me you've seen
the jackdaw's feathers rising from black on black,
the grey snow of its pate and cruel corvid beak,
the seasonal familiar.

Their grandchild, my grandmother,
could always predict death to the hour
but had less luck on the horses.
She left me a keepsake, an oak box
containing cotton swabs, small tools of silver and amber,
a pile of old pennies for covering eyes.

TRAVELLING

after Rebecca Tantony

I point at the wolf moon, hanging large and obvious
at the corner of the windscreen. 'Yes,' you say, 'that's lovely.'
Then: 'That's lovely, look, is that the moon?'

I know that your hair is doubly silvered by the moonlight.
I'm driving you home from getting your hearing aids fixed.
Our conversations slip and slide. I point at the wolf moon.

LAPSE

A tiny rubber has been taken to your brain,
erasing the inner syllables of words
and the connections between them.

Destroying cells,
swiping coherence.

You pause in the middle of your flow;
your flickering eyes halt,
are faded blue and beached.

LEGEND

He was the dandelion puff
blown too close to the flame,
blown away to burn,

all his light-born grace
frazzled,
then destroyed.

She loved him
for the silk kiss
he planted on her dry lips.

She loved him
but swallowed the words
and sealed them in.

She let him go
before he held her;

he slipped from her life
like tugged silk
or water.

It took no effort at all
and she was landlocked for years.

When she met his family
his death had become a healed scar,
a palimpsest of silver stitches,
a clutch of anecdotes
repeated less and less.

WONDER

MIDWIFE

Whose hands?
Invisible in centuries,
capable, clean.
Whose breath?
Breathes with the first breath.
Whose voice?
Soothing, stern
orchestrator of flow.

It's the sister,
mother, grandmother,
witch, widow from down the road.
The invisible woman
who knows that birth comes
with bitter herbs and pain.

Joy is delivered and put on hold
while cords are cut and flesh is stitched,
blood and fluids are washed away,
small mouths are latched to tender teats,
pressure of gums serrates like teeth.

Who places her arm
around fatigued shoulders,
soothes and strengthens, heals,
on a monochrome day
when the sky is a shawl soggy with weeping?
Who is in the background,
central though outside the circle?

Anon.
Every birth should come
with the midwife's name tied to the ankle.
Written in dashing golden script,
an artist's signature.

ANACHRONISTIC ELEGY

i.m. Leonard Cohen

after the storm
moon waxed full
quieted the voice
to a deeper hue

tea in Morocco
goodbye echo

youth flew away
turned fledgling
to crow ——
whisper to gravel
candle to gutter

angel and devil
sang in you —.

WHAT RUMI GAVE ME

after Pascale Petit

all through autumn imagery of sickle moons indigo skies
roses dropping blood petals onto unforgiving soil

in the hallway at night I smelled fresh leather
the departing whiff of camel dung

I dreamt of walking in a desert
fitting my feet into the imprint of rope sandals

the words of Rumi taken like stones from the pool
of original language pure expression naked

AT THE EDGE OF THE TYPHOON

you cotton coverlet your ears against darkness
                              ritual guides you here
in the steamy bathroom
                              a towel licks your back like a dog's tongue

fur is essential to stave off darkness
                              you seem to hug the toy bear
but the bear hugs you

in the mountains
                              monkeys with red faces
sneak down into the shining mirrors of paddy fields
                              they run into gardens
steal apples and plums juice spurts
they hold the fruit against their chins
                              with precise, arching fingers

on screen   and in the temples
and once a year at school   there are Monsters

the wind is the breath of a monster
random colours chime   and fill the paper cheeks of the house
until your dreams shatter   delicate as pastry

your eyes beetle-crush the darkness
in the wide bed where you sleep   with your family
breathing balances the wind's moan
        the bear hugs you for comfort
nothing is certain everything is certain

the star at the window
        pine forest spreading its jagged rug
over the mountains, the morning

ROUND ROBIN

Time ticks too quickly.
You were the girl with sun-blonde hair
and the surfer boyfriend.
We chatted as the tea mashed
in the communal kitchen
on an afternoon that smelled of weed.

Turn around
and we are filling in decades
like colours on a map,
walking looped circles
on the coastal path
to the hot chocolate café
as boats trace an arc
in the sea below the cliffs.

You lent me a book
with the word *Hedgehog*
in the title
and I think of you every time
I look at the unread books on the shelf,
and your kindness
in meeting me at the pub car park
to save me from panic driving
in steep and twisty Cornish lanes.

And now your letter
        with 'news' to friends far and near.
Is this how the future will be?
Banishing sad face
and raising a glass
which somehow catches your sparkle
across the years.

WHEN I MET MINE...

An entire childhood becomes a marble
rolled behind a sofa.
I reach across a desk for a pen
and break a conversation about eyes
held in a fixed gaze and shining.

I think of cats, but this is about
birth mothers.
We met in the car-park at Golden Valley;
we couldn't stop looking at each other.
The second woman says,
I wore a velvet jumpsuit when I met mine for the first time.

I home in on the story, intrusive as a florist styling a petal.
I hate the feel of velvet, the first woman says,
and the talk turns to textures
and the sound a chair makes when it scrapes across the floor.

Some things are just too skinless to talk about
on a Wednesday afternoon when the phones
are waiting to be answered.

SPIROGRAPH

a child unwraps her present
on birthday morning
plastic filters in neon and rose
like vintage aviator glasses
inserts her pen
starts patterns of   not quite repetition
scrawls from neatness
explores distortion

my friend says *Spirograph*
but he means *spirometry*
the measurement of breath
in lungs that are losing function

Saturn's hard return takes thirty years
our bodies replenish in seven
I'm moving out of reminiscence row
as the wheel of change becomes a spiral

I.M. BARBARA HEPWORTH

My fingers scoped mute wisdom of curves,
        sifted air and granite.

I made sculpted eggs at first – a handhold,
        miniature and polite.

My body was a soft chintz – hair caught in a snood.
        I smiled a lot, played paper to my lover's pen.

He tempered me, impregnated my chalk bones,
        first my fire child, then the three,

wood, stone, metal,
        filled my belly with their shifting silver weight.

Time chiselled my face, hawk eyes, hook nose.
        I was mother witch, my work

seen always in relation to the other
        as if inspiration could only flow male to female.

Rolling up my Yorkshirewoman's sleeves,
        hands on and hammer blow,

my body's weight behind each strike;
        each thrilling stroke revealed what is there

when everything is taken away. Grief
        brought me a forest of dark wood.

I carved my anger, sliced and scarred,
        daily toil repeated.

I stood at the foot of a mountain,
        made my garden studio.

I orchestrated teams of men to make
my monumental shapes.

I buffed the tiny cracks of imperfection;
my skin grew spider naevi.

I knew I'd lost more than I could ever gain;
intimacy was a shining stone,

each surface primed and
open to the elemental force of sun and rain.

When fire came the horror charred my ravished body,
left my life's work standing,

wood, stone, metal, the three my legacy
of transformation.

ACKNOWLEDGEMENTS

With heartfelt thanks and gratitude to Bridget Hart and Clive Birnie at Burning Eye for their confidence in me and their encouragement. To Lucy English, Katy Evans-Bush and Bristol Stanza group for helping me shape this book. Also to workshops at the Poetry School online and with Helen Moore. A huge debt to Roddy Lumsden and Glenn Carmichael who are greatly missed. Performance nights including Satellite of Love, Torriano Meeting House, Shine so Hard, Catweazle , Dodo Modern Poets and many others have also been invaluable in helping me make these poems. Most of all, and included in the above - the wide-ranging and variously connected community of poets and writers.

Some of these poems were previously published in *Witches, Warriors and Workers* - A Culture Matters Anthology, *Messing up the Paintwork* - a tribute to Mark E Smith published by Penguin Random House, *Calyx* - a Bristol Stanza anthology and online at *In-between Hangovers*.

Lightning Source UK Ltd.
Milton Keynes UK
UKHW010133160920
369960UK00001B/94